RICKY'S BIG WEEK

By Greg Charpentier

Illustrated by Peet Tamburino

Ricky's Big Week. Copyright © 2019 Greg Charpentier. Produced and printed by Stillwater River Publications. All rights reserved. Written and produced in the United States of America. This book may not be reproduced or sold in any form without the expressed, written permission of the authors and publisher.

Visit our website at www.StillwaterPress.com for more information.

First Stillwater River Publications Edition

ISBN-13: 978-1-950-33945-7

1 2 3 4 5 6 7 8 9 10
Written by Greg Charpentier
Illustrated by Peet Tamburino
Published by Stillwater River Publications, Pawtucket, RI, USA.

The views and opinions expressed in this book are solely those of the author and do not necessarily reflect the views and opinions of the publisher.

The DENTIST!

I hate the chair!

Odd tools are scattered everywhere!

Mom, I can't go to that place,

I can feel my heart begin to race!

A HAIRCUT?

I already got one; it was just last year!

How can you put your son through all
　　this fear?

I won't sit still, I'll squirm—I'll feel the need,

He'll slip and he'll cut me!

I don't want to bleed!

A PLAY DATE?

Mom, you know me, you know what I hate!

It's making new friends at another play date!

A PRESCHOOL PARTY!

We'll have to sing; we'll have to dance!

I'll go into a trance! I'll poop my pants!

Can't I skip this whole week?
Just stay in bed and sleep?

I wish I was at the bottom of the ocean,
Like a rock, still and bedded.
Just *thinking* about this week has got
 me feeling lightheaded!

All of these plans you keep on dismissing.
There's a whole lot of fun that you're certainly missing!

I can't just cancel this schedule we've made.
Life doesn't stop because you *think* you're afraid.

These are the places that we have to go.

Try not to invent outcomes that you can't possibly know.

I'm telling the truth! You don't have to hide.

What is scary to you, only you can decide.

You can hide away from it and sit in your fear.

Or come with me and face it; to make it all disappear!

It's like when a spider lands on your arm.

You flinch and you jerk because you think there is harm.

Nine times out of ten it is a false alarm.

The same will be true for what we must do.

Wipe away your tears, let's face our fears.

TODAY can be the day that they all go away.

I went to the dentist. At first I was scared.

But with the tools my mom gave me I was better **PREPARED**.

Even though I was nervous I decided to stay.

Facing my fears made my fears go away!

So my haircut went **GREAT!**
It finally looks straight!

I went to the party.
I made a new **FRIEND.**

I guess after all my mom was **RIGHT**
   in the end!

The best advice, I can now provide

Is we don't have to fear those feelings inside.

What scares me now, only I will decide.

ABOUT THE AUTHOR

Gregory Charpentier lives in Cranston, Rhode Island and is a father, veteran, and public servant. He graduated from Providence College with honors and is currently in a graduate program studying to become a licensed mental health counselor. His goal is to pursue the endeavor of creating a series of children's books that will reframe the way children are affected by inevitable stressors. The collective quality of life seems to be more disturbed than ever by mental illness, and his intent is to do what he can about that.

Made in the USA
Lexington, KY
12 November 2019